Thomas Holford

The Cave of Neptune

A Dramatic Poem

Thomas Holford

The Cave of Neptune
A Dramatic Poem

ISBN/EAN: 9783744710039

Printed in Europe, USA, Canada, Australia, Japan

Cover: Foto ©Thomas Meinert / pixelio.de

More available books at **www.hansebooks.com**

THE

CAVE OF NEPTUNE;

A

DRAMATIC POEM:

*On the Victory gained by the English Fleet, under
the Command of Lord Howe, in* 1794.

NEPTUNE,	MERCURY,
TRITON,	IRIS,

CHORUS OF NEREIDS.

Arva novâ Neptunia cæde rubescunt. VIRG.

LONDON:

PRINTED BY T. BURTON, NO. 31, LITTLE QUEEN-STREET,
LINCOLN'S-INN FIELDS.

1799.

INVOCATION

TO THE

HARROW MUSES,

TO DEFEND THE USE OF THE HEATHEN
MYTHOLOGY IN POETRY.

Sunt superis sua Iura. OVID.

FAIR sisters of the song, whose earliest strains
In wild Arcadia charm'd the list'ning swains,
Who thence the fruitful seeds of learning bore
Across the ocean to the Latian shore,
There too disturb'd, have turn'd your wand'ring feet   5
To this green isle—here fix'd your lasting seat,

A 2

Who now on Thames's banks near Windsor, stray,
Now on the forked top of Harrow play,
As oft through Tempe's shades ye us'd to range,
Oft shady Tempe for Parnassus change,   10
To him, whom once ye own'd, your favour lend,
And still the lessons, which ye taught, defend.

 At your command how often have I sung,
On Harrow's hill, the race from Saturn sprung—
The God, who dwells in clouds above the sky,   15
Launch'd by whose arm the winged lightnings fly;
The Power, whose trident shakes the solid plain,
Or calms, at will, the terrors of the main;
The King, whose rule, remov'd from mortal sight,
Obey the spectres in the realms of night,   20
And tremble at his frown, and shriek with wild affright.
And am I told, that these must now give place?
That from my page their names I must efface?
Dismiss each God and Goddess from my rhymes
As the dull tale of long-forgotten times?—   25
'Tis yours, ye Nine, to rule each vocal shade,
And who your reign shall venture to invade?
Who bid your vot'ry form his voice anew,
Nor more repeat, what erst he learn'd from you?—

Is then forgot the memorable end 30
Of the rash maids,* who dar'd with you contend?
Or doth it raise no fear, lest all who dare
Like them, like them, transform'd, should wing the air?
Quick, snatch the lyre, to which ye oft have sung,
And shew the world, it needs not be new-strung; 35
Whether ye tell of Ceres, as of old,
Or chuse some other story yet untold;
Let mortals all, who hear the heavenly strain,
Know, that old Saturn's progeny still reign
In Fancy's flow'ry realms and Fiction's wide domain. 40
   Not in my cup, I swear by Styx's lake,
One drop of Lethe's waters will I take;
I will not from remembrance blot the lays,
Which Harrow eccho'd in my younger days—
Those days, in which your subjects lov'd to rove 45
Through the dark windings of the sacred grove; †

---

* The daughters of Pierus contended with the Muses for their
dominions; those Goddesses, having overcome their antagonists,
turned them into birds. The greater part of the song, by which
this victory was atchieved, relates to Ceres.—*Vide* Ovid's Metam.
lib. 5.

† The Grove was the name of a garden at Harrow, in which the
upper boys were allowed by the owner to walk.

Or where the steeple rises to the view,
Or where, in earlier times, the arrow flew ;
Then oft, upon some bank, from sorrow free,
Or at the roots we sat of some old tree,   50
There hail'd the flocks and herds, that wander'd nigh,
Or hymn'd the rosy hours, that fleeted by.
As yet our youthful passions were not strong,
And few the opportunites of wrong ;
But rash Adventures (when th' appointed bound   55
Our feet o'erleapt, and trod forbidden ground),
Or Themes in haste perform'd (an heinous crime),
Or Verse unfinish'd at the stated time
Soon follow'd punishment; nor, that once o'er,
The fault, which caus'd it, was remember'd more.   60
Past scenes ! which, while in manhood we pursue
Life's toilsome march, with fondness we review ;
Now constant care fills up the present hour
With schemes for future wealth, and distant pow'r :
Now if we pass in idleness the day,   65
Or from our road, allur'd by pleasure, stray,

---

* A place on Harrow-Hill called the Buts, where the ceremony
of shooting for the arrow was performed, before that custom was
abolished, and the speeches instituted in its stead.

Stern conscience frowns, an unrelenting foe,
Holds her dread scourge on high, but still delays the blow.
   But whither dost thou tend my lyre? 'tis thine
To sooth our woes, not teach us to repine;   70
'Tis thine, in fairest flowers and myrtle drest,
To calm the tumult of the troubl'd breast:
With skilful hand the chords Arion swept,
Then to the stormy billows fearless leapt,
With ease the list'ning Dolphin * he bestrode,   75
And on his scaly back in triumph rode:
Still, as he pass'd, the sounding harp he bore,
The seas grew calm, the winds forgot to roar,
Till the sweet bard in safety reach'd the shore.
If then, O lyre! thy tones can thus assuage   80
The tempest's wrath, and still old Ocean's rage,
Well may thy sound compose the mind to peace,
Hush every grief, and bid each murmur cease:
Unworthy he to touch thy sacred strings,
Who thinks of care or sorrow, while he sings.   85

---

* Arion being about to be thrown from his ship into the sea, by his companions, in order that they might possess his wealth, obtained leave to play first upon his harp; after a few tunes, he leapt into the waves, and was carried safe to shore by a Dolphin, whom his music had attracted.—*Vide* Ovid, Fast. lib. 2.

THE

CAVE OF NEPTUNE.

SCENE.—Neptune's Cave at the Bottom of the Sea.

ARGUMENT.

NEPTUNE *is sitting at the entrance of his palace—The Nereids enter in confusion, alarmed at an unusual noise, by which they represent themselves to have been disturbed in their cell, where one of them was relating to the rest the story of the Creation.—Neptune says he has already sent a Triton to inquire into the cause of the tumult, and encourages them to resume the song.—The Nereids sing the*

Division of the World between Jupiter, Neptune, and Pluto, enlarging upon the praises of Neptune's share, the Ocean.— The Triton then enters, with intelligence that the sounds they had heard, had been occasioned by a sea-fight between the English and a fleet bearing an unknown flag ; that the engagement, though favourable to the English, had not been decisive, and that he left both parties preparing to renew the contest.—Neptune blames the folly of Man in perverting navigation into the means of annoying his own species ; and the Chorus expose the injustice of his complaints, in respect to the shortness of human life, which has been abridged in its general duration by his own intemperance, and is frequently, as in the present instance, abruptly terminated by his violence. The reflections of the Chorus are interrupted by the noise of the second engagement; the Vengeur is seen to sink at a distance, and the Chorus express their indignation at the pollution offered to the sea.—The Chorus now see Mercury descending through the waters ; on being sent to by Neptune he enters and relates that the fleet, engaged with the English, is from Gaul.—A long conversation ensues between Neptune and Mercury, upon the overthrow of the ancient monarchy of France, and the nature and tendency of the principles, which have given rise to the new state of things in that country, and to the present war.—After informing Neptune

B

that the victory was still undecided, when he left the air, Mercury departs to execute the office, on which he came down, viz. to collect the shadows of the slain, and conduct them to the realms below; and the Chorus sing the difference between Philosophy, (the Daughter of Momus and a Mortal,) ever prompting to new experiments, and Wisdom the Offspring of Jove.—Iris next enters with a message from Jupiter, desiring Neptune to rise in his car, and assist the English fleet; Neptune at first refuses, expressing a determination not to interfere in a contest between mortals; being, however, informed, that his assistance is not required against the Gauls, who are already defeated, but to repress the violence of Æolus, who has let loose his storms, and is opposing the return of the conquerors to their native land, he consents to lend his aid, and accounts for the hatred borne to the English by Æolus, as proceeding from his old enmity against Æneas, from whom they are descended.—The Chorus describe the preparations for the ascent, declare their intention of hastening the progress of the victorious fleet homeward, and conclude with the mention of the joy with which it will be received on its arrival in England.

SCENE.—Neptune's Cave at the Bottom of the Sea.

Neptune sitting at the entrance of the Cave—enter to him the Nereids.

NEPTUNE.

SAY, wherefore, Daughters, thus, in wild dismay
To my old mansion have ye urg'd your way?
Your scatter'd hair and trembling eyes proclaim,
Without the aid of language, that ye came

Upon no slight occasion ; quickly speak,   5
Why thus hath fled the coral from your cheek?
Have my rude Tritons any insult dar'd?
Or by the surly Proteus are ye scar'd,
Driving his scaly herds too near the cell,
In which my blue-eye'd daughters love to dwell?   10
Without reserve declare your sad distress,
Your sire and king shall quickly grant redress.

NEREID.

We thank thee, Father, often in our grief
In thy protection have we found relief.—
No insult from rude Tritons we sustain,   15
Nor of old Proteus come we to complain ;
Far from his herds we sat, within the cell,
In which thy blue-ey'd daughters love to dwell ;
The nymph Ligea * to her sisters told, .
How this fair world from chaos rose of old ;   20
When, as we listen'd to the pleasing tale,
Dread noises, all at once, our ears assail ;
Like thunder, much they seem'd, but seem'd more nigh
Than thunder when it bellows through the sky.

---

* Ligea one of the Nereids, so called from the sweetness of her voice.

Scar'd at the horrid din, our helpless bands   25
Forsook the Cave, and fled along the sands:
Nor ceas'd our flight, until our weary feet
Had reach'd the entrance of this sacred seat.
Chear'd by thy presence, still we dread to hear
What dire event impends; nor vain our fear—   30
For never, since by thy all-powerful aid
The strong foundations of the deep were laid,
Were heard such noises in these realms before.

NEPTUNE.

DAUGHTERS, myself did hear the dread uproar.
Tremendous was the sound; the palace-wall   35
Shook as it eccho'd through the vaulted hall:
Nor know I yet the cause; but stay ye here,
My trembling Children, and compose your fear;
For I have sent a Triton, to inquire
What meant the tumult: strike, meanwhile, the lyre,   40
And let my wat'ry subjects all rejoice
To hear the music of Ligea's voice!

CHORUS.

STROPHE.

Soon * as the Gods repos'd (their labours done),
In his flaming car, the Sun
Rush'd through the vault of heaven, as if in haste   45
To view the glories of his new domain,
Rending the veil of darkness, as he pass'd;
The world's great fabric stood at once display'd;
Amidst their gazing train
Well pleas'd, old Saturn's sons survey'd   50
The wond'rous pile their hands had made;
And as beneath their comprehensive view
The vast expanse in three divisions lay,   .
Three lots at once the mighty Brothers drew
Fixing to endless time the limits of their sway.   55

ANTISTROPHE.

To Jove was given the empire of the sky;
There he sits in majesty,

---

* The Nereid is supposed to resume the song, which was inter-
rupted, and the Creation of the world having been described (as
appears by the 19th and 20th lines) she now proceeds to sing the
Division of it.

In the bright regions of eternal day;
Among the clouds, that bear his massy throne
Loud thunders roll, and forked lightnings play.   60
'Twas Pluto's doom to rule the shades below :
Far from the Gods, alone,
Within the sable realms of woe
Where Styx's sullen waters flow,
He sways his iron sceptre ; by his side,   65
Snatch'd from her sisters of ætherial race,
Persephone, a melancholy bride,
Beholds in silent awe the horrors of the place.

EPODE.

MIGHTY Ruler of the sea,
Blest be the lot, which gave these realms to thee.—   70
Propitious Chance thy empire laid,
Nor in eternal shade,
Nor in the kingdoms of unceasing light;
For o'er our grots and caves the Night
Her sable mantle throws,   75
What time th' empyreal coursers close
Their eager race, with furious leap,
Bounding down the western steep,

Till their burning sides they lave
In the cool Atlantic wave; ·   80
And when the Hours unbar the eastern gate,
And to th' admiring world the God of day
Marches forth in gorgeous state,
Here too his orb is seen;
Not blazing with the yellow glare,   85
With which he fires the regions of the air;
Our waters blunt his arrows keen,
Slow through the wave descends the broken ray,
And decks our chrystal seats in tints of softest green.
What though oft the wintry storm,   90
Sweeping furious through the skies,
With many a wrinkle, as it flies,
Ocean's hoary face deform?
The great Abyss doth undisturb'd repose;
Though Æolus should wide unclose   95
His bolts and bars, releasing every wind
In his vast cave confin'd,
The blust'ring Hosts would seek in vain
To dive into the main,
And violate the bosom of the deep.   100
Sisters, in security
In our grottos we may lie,

And woo with softest songs the God of sleep;
Or, sitting on some moss-grown steep,
Count the fish, that frolic by :   105
Or will ye rather in the waters play ?
Or chuse ye on the yellow sands to stray ?
Or among the rocks to go,
Where the spreading Corals grow,
And pull their branches to adorn our Cell,   110
Mix'd with many a pearly shell ?
Let not terrors vain alarm us;
Nothing in these realms can harm us.
But see the Triton messenger appears,
Quick, Father, bid him speak, and say what caus'd our
    fears.   115

Enter Triton.

NEPTUNE.

Much I commend thy haste, my Son, declare
What saw'st thou in the Regions of the Air ?

TRITON.

Obedient to thy Voice, my Sire, I sped
Quick through the yielding waters, till my head

c

Into thin air I rais'd, then look'd on high,   120
Whence came the dread disturbance to descry;
Clear shone the azure vault of Heav'n around,
And not a spot on the vast arch I found
To dim the shining lustre of the day :
But at some distance on the waters lay   125
A thick white mist, not in the air it hung,
But to the surface of the Ocean clung.
From out the hollow bosom of that cloud
The noise, thou heard'st, proceeded; not more loud
Roar'd the dread thunder, when the Giants strove   130
To drag from his great throne celestial Jove,
When by his bolts, transfix'd, Typhöeus fell
From high Olympus to the gulphs of Hell:
Here too I saw the livid lightning flash,
And ever and anon an horrid crash   135
Reach'd my astonish'd ear; so (when the roar
Of the wild tempest rises on the shore,
When the grove shakes upon the lofty rock,
And its tall oaks against each other knock,)
Resound the waters, if some loosen'd tree   140
Down the steep cliff is dash'd into the sea.
Mix'd with these sounds I heard a bitter cry,
'Twas the sad voice of Human Misery;

The groan of thousands rent the troubl'd air,
Dire screams of pain, and ravings of despair: 145
With these, the clamour loud of savage joy,
And shouts of men exulting to destroy ;
The wild uproar of strife, and din of war,
That howl around the fierce Bellona's car.
Full well 1 then perceiv'd, that hostile rage 150
Had urg'd the sons of Earth in fight t' engage
Upon our wat'ry plains ;—Distain'd with blood,
High on their floating towers the warriors stood,
Thence hurl'd destruction on each other's head,
And strew'd each adverse ship with heaps of dead ; 155
Tore down its proud aspiring mast, or gave
Through its pierc'd sides an entrance to the wave.

NEPTUNE.

But say, what mighty power did they employ,
·Across the sea to spread such fierce annoy ?
How from a distance thus each other reach ? 160
How through those wooden bulwarks force a breach ?
Thick planks of sturdy oak the ship surround,
Whence e'en the surging billows back rebound.

C 2

TRITON.

A wond'rous engine did the means supply,
A hollow Tube, within whose cavity   165
Were kindl'd fires; these, struggling for a vent,
Large iron bolts with force Volcanic sent
Far as the eye could reach, athwart the air;
And as the flames did thus a passage tear
From their deep womb, they gave that horrid roar   170
Which to thine ear the troubled waters bore.

But nought distinctly, while the battle rag'd,
Could I discern; in distant fight engag'd,
Some ships now dimly through the mist appear'd;
But, as they nearer to each other steer'd,   175
They pour'd their fury with redoubl'd might,
And thicker shades soon snatch'd them from my sight.

At length the tumult of the conflict ceas'd,
Silence prevail'd; at her return well-pleas'd,
In calm repose, the Air and Ocean lay;   180
The clouds of smoke roll'd heavily away,
And two great Navies stood disclos'd to view,
Retiring one, one eager to pursue.
The latter quickly by her flag I knew,

The flag so oft by Albion's sons display'd,   185
As to our Ocean's utmost bounds they trade :
But that, which further contest had declin'd,
Unknown I left; three colours were combin'd
In equal stripes her pennant to compose,   190
Red, White, and Blue, beside each other rose ;
But since Man's restless mind, or hopes of gain,
First bade him wander o'er the pathless main,
Though on our waves his ships have met mine eyes,
In number as the Stars that deck the skies,   195
Yet ne'er 'mongst all the various flags they bore
Saw I that ensign on the Seas before :
Vainly it seem'd to woo the tardy wind,
The British Fleet came pressing on behind;
And both for farther contest 'gain prepare,   200
When swiftly I descended from the air,
These tidings to thine ear, mine honour'd Sire, to bear.

NEPTUNE.

Of all the creatures Jove design'd to bless,
And sent on earth in search of happiness,
Mankind, who boast their more extensive view,   205
The way least see ; or seeing, least pursue.

Each blessing which the fav'ring Gods bestow,
Their foolish passions make the source of woe.
Minerva deign'd to guide the builder's hand,
And Argo * rose upon the Grecian Strand ;   210
Thence as the vessel wander'd o'er the deep,
My voice propitious bade the tempests sleep ;
The barriers thus, by Nature interpos'd,
Between Earth's different regions we unclos'd ;
Led wond'ring man, to realms before unknown,   215
To learn new arts, and make their fruits his own :
Then Commerce hasten'd from her golden store,   )
With bounteous hand large streams of wealth to pour,   }
And mighty cities rose on many a barren shore.   )
But had I known that Mortals would employ,   220
Perversely thus, each other to destroy,
The means we gave their welfare to increase,
And with their broils disturb'd my kingdom's peace—
This had I known; when first her lofty sail
The vessel spread, and flew before the gale,   225
One swelling wave had burst upon her head,
And all her crew been number'd with the dead ;

---

* *Argo* was the name of the ship in which the Argonauts made
their famous expedition—it is always mentioned among the Greeks
as the first ship, *i. e.* the first vessel with sails.

The crowds, which loudly chear'd her rapid flight,
Had shriek'd, as she went down, with wild affright,
Nor Man again had dar'd to tempt the Ocean's might. 230

CHORUS.

STROPHE.

Oft at the dead and silent hour of night,
When from our grottos deep, and dusky caves,
To the calm surface of the seas we rise,
To gaze upon the pale Moon's silver light,
Or count the stars, that wander through the skies ;   235
Mix'd with the murmur of the breaking waves,
From distant shores the tranquil Air
Slowly to my ear doth bear
The mournful accents of complaining Man :
Rash he upbraids to Nature's plan,   240
    " That ere his eyes behold the light of day,
" Death marks him for his prey ;
" That first the new-born infant to assail
" Disease the Tyrant sends and pain,
" With all their horrid train ;   245
" That, if these cruel ministers are slow
" Against health's stubborn vigour to prevail,
" Danger, then, and many a snare

" Across life's narrow path the Foe doth lay
" To catch the hapless traveller on his way,   250
" And drag him to the tomb, that yawns below :
" That vain his toil, and useless is his care,
" For man is seldom doom'd to wear
" The wreath, in youth he gain'd, on age's silver hair."

ANTISTROPHE.

CEASE, Mortals, cease! nor thus with voice prophane 255
Charge on impartial Heav'n the ills, ye feel;
The world first made, Jove plac'd the Sisters three
Deep in those realms, where shades eternal reign,
There bade them deal the dole of destiny.
One holds the Distaff, and One turns the Wheel,   260
The wheel, which doth for ever run ;
.And as the vital Thread is spun,
The Third surveys it with unerring eye,
Holding the iron Shears on high ;
Till once her hand doth on the work descend,   265
And then man's life doth end.
But long of old the mighty Power delay'd
To smite the Skein, nor seem'd, as now,
In haste to strike the blow ;
Till Man provok'd the patient deity,   270

Forsook the verdant lawn and sunny glade,
Where with Fawns, and Satyrs gay,
And the brown Wood-Nymph Health he us'd to roam;
Sought walled cities and the gilded dome,
Where dwells the soft Enchantress Luxury;   275
And there in Pleasure's downy lap he lay,
And slumber'd through the live-long day,
Nor heeded, as he slept, his strength did pass away.

EPODE.

For soon the Flood of Life, which erst supplied,
Warm through the glowing veins its salient tide,   280
Blush'd in the cheek, and sparkl'd in the eyes,
And swiftly round its mazy circle ran,
Chill'd by the icy hand of Sloth, began
To slack its course, and by degrees more slow
It crept along the winding arteries,   285
Till scarce the lazy stream appear'd at all to flow.
—Then dire Disease first shook Man's languid frame,
And with her came
Sad Melancholy, gloomy Discontent,
With all the dark and visionary Train   290
Of shapeless Terrors, that a passage find
Through the disorder'd senses to the mind:

D

And pining Sorrow, Fear, and Shame,
With Envy e'er on mischief bent,
And Hate, and Anger fierce, the monstrous brood of
    Pain.   295
—Why then of Heaven doth mortal Man complain?
On his own head he drew an early doom,
And open'd for himself the tomb,
Ere Nature bade him quit the stage;
And ever and anon with frantic rage   300
He swells the note of war aloud,
Till at the call whole Nations crowd,
To dip their guilty hands in human gore—

SEMI-CHORUS.

And hark! e'en now the horrid Thunders roar;
The Storm of Death again   305
Is rising on the main.

SEMI-CHORUS.

Rash Mortals!—Dread ye not the Elean fate, *
While thus the shafts of Jove ye emulate?

---

* *Elean Fate.*—Salmoneus, king of Elis, built a bridge over
the city, along which he drove his chariot to imitate thunder,
throwing down burning torches for lightning.—He was struck by

—A real bolt the God from far
Threw with a tremendous sound,   310
The Monarch tumbl'd from his car,
A blacken'd Corse, upon the ground.

SEMI-CHORUS.

HARKEN, Sisters, now the roar
I's louder than before;
And, see, a mighty Mass is downward borne,   315
The yielding waves beneath its weight divide,
'Tis an huge Vessel in the conflict torn;
Behold upon its masts, and on its side,
Are crowds of dying Men: Their cries
Reach not our ears: The shriek   320
Of mortal voices is too weak
To pierce our watery fluid; but your eyes
May see the Wretches vainly gasp for breath,
And struggle in the pangs of death.

Jupiter with lightning for his impiety—See 6th Book of Virgil, in
which he is mentioned among the criminals seen by Æneas in the
infernal regions.

D 2

CHORUS.

GREAT Jove, within their native regions keep   325
These sons of Earth ; There let them load the plain
(If blood be their delight) with heaps of slain ;
But let not foul Pollution stain
Our chrystal Vaults serene, and Temples of the Deep.

SEMI-CHORUS.

SOME God from Air, my Sisters, downward bends   330
IIis course, and swiftly through our waves descends.

SEMI-CHORUS.

'TIS Mercury, Caduceus * in his hand
IIe bears, and now his feet have reach'd the sand.

NEPTUNE.

Go, Triton, to him quick our greeting bear,
And bid him to this spot with speed repair ;   335
Say, Ocean's king his presence doth require.

                          [*Triton goes out.*

SEMI-CHORUS.

THY Summons he obeys, mine honour'd sire.

                          [*Looking out.*

---

* The name of Mercury's wand. ·

Enter Mercury.

NEPTUNE.

'Tis well—Hail son of Maia and of Jove,
What hither brings thee from the realms above?
Loud Tumult in the air hath long prevail'd;   340
E'en here the horrid Din our ears assail'd,
Disturb'd the silence of my peaceful reign
Here, in the deep recesses of the main.
Nor know we yet, what thus hath mortals led
To pour their vengeance on each others head;   345
The Cause relate; but first say, who the Foes,
That in the contest Albion's sons oppose?
For, as I hear, their fleet an Ensign wore,
Which on our seas was ne'er unfurl'd before.

MERCURY.

The foes of Albion's sons from Gallia came,   350
A land long noted in the rolls of Fame;
On her few ships of late strange Colours fly,
But oft her well-known vessels met thine eye,
When from her ports to many a distant shore
Her busy trade the Flower-de-Luces bore.   355

NEPTUNE.

FAIR France of old I know, her wide Domains,
Her crowded Cities, and her fertile Plains :
But what this dreadful conflict hath brought on
Between her Fleet and mighty Albion ?

MERCURY.

GREAT King, who far beneath the sounding wave   360
Hast fixed thy seat in Ocean's silent cave ;
Yet oft dost view the Earth's extended plain,
Borne in thy floating car upon the main ;
Much wilt thou feel of Anger and Surprise,
When next the Realms above shall meet thine eyes : 365
France is no more.   A crimson Stain of blood
Marks the sad spot, where once her empire stood :
The mighty Monarch, who her sceptre bore,
A headless trunk, lies weltering in his gore :
Driv'n from the much-lov'd soil, which gave them birth, 370
Her gallant Nobles wander o'er the earth,
While furious crowds at home with frantic cry
Prophane the sacred name of Liberty ;
Spurn at all laws, and by no rule restrain'd,
Spread havock and destruction through the land.   375

For crimes of blackest die the Public weal
Is made pretext; beneath the mask of Zeal,
Revenge and Malice hunt their helpless prey;
And Murder walks abroad in open day.
As once by Cadmus charm'd, the * Theban band,   380
Each raising 'gainst the rest his armed hand,
(A monst'rous prodigy) by mutual blows
Fell to the parent earth from whence they rose,
So Gallia's sons had press'd ere now the plain,
In civil discord by each other slain,   385
But that their Leaders, trembling at th' event
Of their own arts, to foreign warfare sent
The thousands, who at home disdain'd controul.
They blew the trump of war, from pole to pole
The blast resounded, 'till its loud alarms   390
Had call'd the Nations of the earth to arms.

---

* Cadmus having lost all his companions, who were destroyed
by a serpent, killed the monster'; and, by the direction of Minerva,
sowed its teeth in the ground—from this seed sprang up a band of
armed men—as Cadmus was preparing to attack these new ene-
mies, they fell upon each other, and fought till only five remained,
who assisted Cadmus in building Thebes. Ovid Metam. lib. 3.—
Another account adds, that this sudden hostility was produced by
a stone thrown among them by Cadmus for that purpose.

:Nor on the seas alone the warriors meet ;
The solid Land too shakes beneath their feet.

NEPTUNE.

Once kindled, far the flames of Discord spread,
.But what in France this horrid mischief bred ?   395

MERCURY.

Since first from earth, at Jove's command he rose,
Man, restless man, could ne'er enjoy repose.
·Of ills he most complains, when most at ease,
And full of health, imagines a disease :.
Or.blest with all, that Heav'n can on him pour,   400
Throws what he hath, away in search of more.
The Monarchy of France from ancient days
Had stood ; the Nation's greatness spake its praise.
Some faults it had, which Wisdom would have cur'd,
Or, ere the system have destroy'd, endur'd ;   405
For let vain Man survey the earth around,
Where will his works without defect be found ?
—Not from its faults arose the Discontent,
Which overthrew that ancient government.   ·
The Arrogance of vain Philosophy   410
Dar'd on the State her baneful schemes to try ;

She spake of grievances, proclaim'd aloud
A list of fancied ills, and told the crowd,
The Fabric, which their rude forefathers priz'd,
Ought by the wiser sons to be despis'd ;   415
Thus making for its ruin a pretence,
Th' antiquity, which prov'd its excellence :
She promis'd in its stead a Pile to raise,
Where all alike in ease should pass their days ;
Nor, while her visionary plan she drew,   420
Man's wants consider'd, or his nature knew.
Strange were her maxims, " That the Sons of earth,
" Sprung from one source, were equal at their birth ;
" That all, what Heaven bestow'd, alike should share,
" Since all alike were Providence's care ;   425
" Nor was it just, his equals Man should see
" Above himself in wealth or in degree."

NEPTUNE.

STRANGE maxims these indeed ! Philosophy
Thus from plain sense and truth doth ever flie
To specious sophistry ; thus ever weaves   430
Her subtle web ; and e'en herself deceives.
There is in Man a Particle of fire
Divine infus'd, which prompts him to aspire :

E

This active power can never be destroy'd;
But may in each be well or ill employ'd;   435
If well-directed, it to Virtue leads:
If ill, to Vice gives birth and foul misdeeds:
Hence wisest Legislators, with deep thought
Framing the social system, e'er have sought
Not to root out, but in its course to guide   440
Ambition, and fit objects to provide
For its pursuit; thus in Communities
Degrees and ranks above each other rise.
And abject is the mind, which at their birth
Would on one level place the sons of earth,   445
And with such niggard hand reward bestow,
That not beyond the grave the stream should flow:
What! in their prospect shall the Good and Great
Be circumscrib'd within life's narrow date,
And comfortless into the earth descend,   450
Griev'd that their Honours with themselves shall end?
No—In the tranquil evening of his days
When pleas'd the Hero thinks on former praise,
And views his well-earn'd Laurels, let him know,
They yet shall flourish on another brow;   455
That, when at rest (his race of glory run)
He sleeps within the tomb, his noble Son,

Grac'd with his titles, shall revive his name,
Tread in his steps, and emulate his fame.
For Wealth—To guard from force the larger share, 460
Acquir'd by toil and labour, the main care
And purpose is of government ; if Men
Were equal all in this, where would be then
The recompense of patient Industry ?
Not on such terms doth Heav'n its gifts supply,   465
The boon bestow'd on Man he should possess,
As may promote the general happiness ;
'Twas given at first his Talents to employ,
And what by those he gains, Heav'n wills him to enjoy.

CHORUS.

In ev'ry Path he treads, or high, or low,   470
Flowers in his road, and Thorns promiscuous grow ;
Still Fortune's temple glitters on his eyes,
And Hope on golden wings before him flies ;
Joyful he follows, where the Goddess leads,
Nor labour, as he mounts, nor danger heeds ;   475
But if henceforward none must strive to gain
The steep ascent, but on one level plain
Without pursuit the Sons of earth shall stray,
What then shall chear them on their dreary way ?

E 2

NEPTUNE.

Yet few there are among mankind, who know,   480
To what their sorrows or their joys they owe.
And discontented many in each State
Will e'er be found, who all above them hate,
And envy those, whom they should emulate.
Say on, my Son, the factious crowd, I fear,   485
To their new Teacher lent a willing ear.

MERCURY.

On every side the People round her throng'd
To hear that wealth and power to them belong'd:
They listen'd to her voice in wild delight,
"Till rouz'd at length to vindicate their right,   490
They heav'd the Monarchy from off its base;
And bade her raise a fabric in its place.
But this no easy task the Goddess found,
And her new Pile soon tumbled to the ground:
Another, quickly on its ruins rose;   495
Now this too shakes, meanwhile in torrents flows,
The nation's dearest blood, and long shall flow;
Successive systems will they yet o'erthrow;

And thousands more must perish in the wreck;
Ere sad Experience shall this phrenzy check: 500
For now the Multitude dominion crave,
And think the man, who shares not pow'r a slave;
Look round with scorn on each well-order'd State,
And in their fury vow eternal hate
To Monarchy, oft threat'ning to pull down
Each neighbour King, and trample on his Crown.   505

NEPTUNE.

But why, when thus they have o'erturn'd the throne
In France, this rage 'gainst foreign Monarchs shewn?

MERCURY.

The Doctrine, they have learn'd, was not design'd
Within the bounds of France to be confin'd.
Philosophy a larger plan pursues,   510
And o'er the peopled earth extends her views;
" Around the globe," she saith, " the gloomy Night
" Of Ignorance prevails o'er Reason's light;
" But soon my hand shall tear the veil away,
" And Man in native Majesty display.   515
" Nor shall he bear, when once himself he knows,
" The load, his present Governors impose,

" But conscious of his strength, throw off his chains,
" And from each tyrant Ruler pluck the reins.
" Torn from their heads, upon the ground shall lie   520
" The ensigns of departed Royalty ;
" While Liberty shall triumph at their fall,
" And man's whole Race to her new Temple call.

NEPTUNE.

But through all ages, since the world began,
In distant realms hath differ'd Man from man ;   525
In manners varying, though the same in kind,
He's here a Savage, there by Arts refin'd ;
Hence diff'rent forms of government arise,
Republics some, and some are Monarchies:
Would then Philosophy's o'er-weening pride   530
One common Scheme of rule for all provide !

MERCURY.

In ev'ry region of the earth, whate'er
His manners, customs, or opinions are,
(Form'd by long habit in successive times,
Or nature's influence in different climes,)   535
Philosophy presumes to think, that Man
Will at her voice become Republican :

At once the Leaders of her frantic crowd
To all the nations round * proclaim'd aloud,
That, ".as in each these maxims should prevail,   540
" And Faction's strength the government assail,
" The Gallic armies would th' insurgents aid,
" Nor Peace with Kings or Nobles should be made."

NEPTUNE.

Did then this insult to all states excite
Brave Albion's sons to cope with them in fight ?   545

MERCURY.

Not this alone; for Albion once destroy'd,
They fear'd no other power; and hence employ'd
Their utmost means to nourish discontent
In that great kingdom 'gainst its government :
They found men there too happy and too wise   550
To listen to their foolish Theories ;
And Albion, not deluded, but alarm'd
By these attempts, in haste her forces arm'd ;
Foil'd in his secret hope the Foe prepar'd
For open force, and War at once declar'd.   555

---

* By the decree of the French Convention, passed 19th Nov. 1792.

NEPTUNE.

Say, now, when gliding downward from the sky
Thou saw'st the fleets, to which did Victory
At length incline ?

MERCURY.

                    Mine eyes did not behold
The adverse ships, for yet the Thunder roll'd,   56
When through the fields of air I wing'd my flight,
And Clouds of smoke conceal'd them from my sight.
But ere I left those regions I perceiv'd
That the broad Sea with rising billows heav'd,
And the fresh Breezes, as they murmur'd by,   56
Gave sullen presage that a storm was nigh.
But now farewel, for I along the sand,*
Must slowly pace ; and with my potent wand
Collect the fleeting shadows of the slain ;
Then lead them to the verge of Pluto's reign,   57

---

* The circumstance of Mercury's being employed in conductin
the souls of the dead to the shades below, with the power of hi
wand over them, is constantly alluded to in the ancient poets.

Where gloomy Charon waits to waft them o'er
The Stygian gulph, which they shall pass no more.

[*Mercury goes out.*

CHORUS.

STROPHE.

Vainest is Momus * of the Gods above,
Who nor the curious pile, Minerva fram'd,
Nor plastic skill of Vulcan would approve;   575
E'en the rare work, thine Hand had made,
Immortal Sire, his rash Presumption blam'd.
To him Philosophy, in times of Yore,
A Mortal bore;
Rejected by the Gods, on earth she roams,   580
Deceives in Wisdom's garb the giddy crowd,
And as her Sire, in censure loud,
Of error talks, and descants on defect;
A mirror in her hand displayed,
Back to the sight distorted doth reflect   585
Each object round, while many a plan

---

* Momus was notorious among the Gods for being dissatisfied
with every thing—A Horse made by Minerva, a Man by Vulcan,
and a Bull by Neptune, were submitted to his inspection, that he
might decide which was the most ingenious contrivance; but
instead of giving judgement he found fault with each of them.

She bears on high, and many a scheme
Drawn by Folly in a dream ;
Yet strong her influence over Man,
And love of change she spreads, where'er she comes :
Fain would her Pride new model e'en the skies,   590
As on she strides, and with presumptuous eyes
Surveys the Heavens round,
But stumbles o'er the stone, that lies upon the ground.

ANTISTROPHE.

FAR different is Wisdom ; she of old
Sprang from the head of Jove, as o'er the flood   595
Of dark Confusion, which in Chaos rolled,
Planning Creation's vast design,
The God in silent meditation stood.
On Helicon's sequester'd top she dwells ;
There, in their Cells,   600
Unheard by mortal ear, the Muses sing
Of every star, that holds its course on high,
And all the wonders of the sky,
And what on earth doth pass from age to age ;
While listening to the strain divine,   605
The Goddess notes it in her sacred page :
Yet often from her high abode,

When mortal voice implores her aid,
Doth descend the heavenly Maid,
And Man, through many a rugged road,   610
Safe to his journeys end her Counsels bring.
With modest gait she walks, and downcast look;
And much she meditates upon her book; -
And often stops t' explore,
Whene'er she treads a path, that was untrod before. 615

SEMI-CHORUS.

CHILDREN of Clovis, round whose youthful brows
Long since the splendor of the Regal Crown
Beamed, like the rising Sun of France's power,
Bidding her smiling realms rejoice
In prospect fair of greatness and renown: 620
'Twas in an evil hour,
That ye mistook for Wisdom's sober voice
The ravings of Philosophy.
The Sun of France, pluck'd madly from his Sphere,
Hath clos'd at once his long career,   625
And quench'd his golden rays
In blood; The spacious Regions, late the scene
Of his bright influence, now shrouded lie
In darkness, black as is the sable wing

F 2

Of Night, or mantle of Hell's ebon Queen;   630
Save when at times the spark of Discord, blown
By the rude breath of wild Democracy,
Flames out with sudden blaze,
And, glaring through surrounding horrors, shews
The headless Image of a murder'd King,   635
And Thousands striving hard for mastery
Amid the Ruins of a fallen Throne.

SEMI-CHORUS.

 FALL'N is the mighty Throne of Charlemain;
The vast Colossus, which for ages past
Had rear'd its giant Head on high,   640
And stood through many a stormy blast,
Amazing the beholders eyes
With its stupendous Size
And wond'rous Symmetry,
O'erthrown by Folly's hand, with heaviest sound   645
Came down; loading the plain,
An awful lesson to the Nations round,
The shapeless mass of desolation lies;
While brooding o'er the pile, the Foe
Of Gods above, and Men below,   650
Sits monstrous Anarchy,

Right glad, in part the sway to have regain'd,
Which in old times he held, when he in Chaos reigned.

SEMI-CHORUS.

See from Jove bright Iris sent,
In the watry Cloud hath bent   655.
Her many-colour'd Bow, whose end
Doth unto the Wave descend;
O'er the Arch behold her run;
Her gay Vest glitters in the sun;
And now she dives into the sea;   660
- Lord of the deep, she comes to thee.

Enter Iris.

NEPTUNE.

Bright Iris hail! what message dost thou bring
From cloud-compelling Jove to Ocean's King!

IRIS.

Thus spake the God; " Go, Daughter of the skies,
" And urge our Brother of the seas to rise   665

" In all his power, Say, Dangers dread impend
" O'er Albion's sons, unless his aid he lend.

NEPTUNE.

Would then your King, that I should interpose
In Human strife, and combat Mortal foes?
Nor so, nor Ocean shall put forth his power,   670
To crush the puny Insect of an hour;
If Albion to the strength of Gaul give way,
Albion must fall; I mix not in the fray.

IRIS.

Not such the wish of Jove, nor Albion's fleet,
Needs aid divine a mortal foe to meet.   675
On its proud ensign e'er I left the sky,
All terrible and grim sat Victory,
As if she long had hovered in the smoke,
Before she lighted on the British oak.
But when, unable to maintain the fight,   680
The ships of Gallia turn'd their prows to flight,

The King of Winds sent forth his strongest gales,
To urge their course ; and fill'd their hoisted sails,
'Till to a friendly port his aid had sped,
Such shattered vessel, that from battle fled,   685
(One sunk in fight, beneath the Ocean lies,
. And six remain the gallant Victor's prize) ;
But the same blast, which bore the Gauls to land,
Drives off the Britons from fair Albion's strand ;
And Æolus still bids the whirlwind sweep,   690
With unrelenting fury o'er the deep ;
Full from the North the raging Tempest blows
Nor can the lab'ring Fleet its force oppose :—
The skilful Pilot to the storm would turn
The Vessel's head, but vainly at the stern   695
The rudder's pow'r attempts her course to guide,
And the big wave bursts frequent on her side:
Mute is the voice of Triumph, late so loud,
And rising cares the Warrior's brow o'ercloud ;
For oft he thinks, amid the Tempest's roar,   700
In silent sadness on his native shore,
And those dear objects he may see no more ;
Yet some, he hopes, shall still survive to tell
Of that great Battle, which they fought so well.

NEPTUNE.

BRAVE are the Sons of Albion, nor shall thus   705
Be made the sport of angry Æolus :
I thought that boist'rous God long since had known
That Ocean's rule belongs to me alone ;
In times of old I warn'd him to restrain
His furious Minions, nor disurb the main   7.10
Without my leave, when eager to destroy,
His rage pursu'd the said remains of Troy ;
And in my car * I rose above the wave,
The great Æneas from his storms to save.
And doth he now again his winds untie ?—   715
Still he pursues his ancient enmity ;
The smother'd flame rekindled at the sight
Of Albion's Navy, triumphing in fight :
For well 'tis known from old Tradition's strains,
That Dardan Blood † still flows in British veins :   720
That when, self-banish'd from the Latian Plain,
His faithful Band of Followers o'er the Main :

---

* See the first Book of Virgil.

† Dardan is Trojan.   Dardanus was an old King of Troy.

Old Brutus, Grandson of Æneas,* led,
(Griev'd for the blood, his erring hand had shed,)
Long worn and tempest-tost, on Albion's Strand:　　725
(Such was the sacred Oracle's command,)
He moor'd his Fleet; and vanquishing the might
Of Gog and Magog, terrible in Fight,
He fix'd his Empire on that fertile shore,
And call'd it Britain from the name he bore.　　730
　　But wherefore do I here consume the hour
In these details? array'd in all my power,
Upon the Ocean will I now go forth;
Soon to his dungeon shall the stormy North
Fly-howling back, nor dare contend with me,　　735
Old Saturn's Son, and Monarch of the Sea.——

---

* It is related, by Geoffry, of Chaucer, an old Historian, as quoted
by Rapin, that soon after the arrival of the Trojans in Italy, Brutus,
having had the misfortune accidentally to kill his father Sylvius, the
son (according to some the grandson) of Æneas, left that country,
and was directed by an Oracle to settle in the Island of Albion;
the History adds, that after experiencing various adventures and
performing many great actions, he landed somewhere on the coast
of Devonshire or Cornwall, defeated the Giants, to whom the Island
was then subject, the chief of whom were Gog and Magog, and
established himself in the country, calling his followers Brutons,
or Britons, and the Land itself Britain.

G

Sons of the deep prepare the car, prepare
To mount with me into the Realms of Air.

SEMI-CHORUS.

STROPHE.

Sons of the Deep, prepare the Car;
And first the brazen gates unbar   740
Of the vast cave, in whose recess it stands
Form'd of old by Vulcan's hands.*
Him on the Lemnian ground,
Where by his fall from Heaven all bruis'd he lay,
Silver-footed Thetis found;   745
And with Eurynome did safe convey,
Beneath the sounding wave, far from the eye of day.
For nine long years within her friendly cell,
Did he in concealment dwell;

---

* The story of Vulcan's fall from Heaven into the Island of
Lemnos, and of the assistance afforded to him on that occasion by
Thetis and Eurynome is related by Vulcan himself in the 18th Book
of the Iliad—He there says that he worked for the two Goddesses
nine years making bracelets, and rings, &c. in the cave concealed
from Gods and Men—he may not improperly be supposed to have
employed part of the time in building Neptune's Car.

And there, at her desire,   750
The Car, which e'en the Gods admire,
For Neptune, powerful king,
The skilful Artist fram'd, a precious offering.
Of Silver is the work, whereon the hand
Of Mulciber * hath labour'd to engrave   755
The Ocean's bed, and every spot of land,
Mountain, and Vale, that lies beneath the wave:
And each Descendant of the Wat'ry Line,
Sea-God and Nymph marine, the skill divine
Hath their contriv'd to place;   760
And these the God so curiously
Hath wrought, that on its near approach, the Eye
The features of each countenance may trace.

SEMI-CHORUS.

ANTISTROPHE.

Draw forth the Car; then on it spread
The Sea-green mantle, which from thread   765
Of twisted weed herself fair Thetis made;
In it hath her Art display'd

---

* Vulcan, so called from softening metal.

The Nations of the Deep,
O'er whom our mighty Sire extends his care,
Some that swim, and some that creep,   770
The Finny brood, oft rising to the Air,
And monstrous Phocæ, wallowing in the sands, are there.
The milk-white Horses from the stalls too lead,
Where they on Ambrosia feed;
Quick o'er them throw the Reins;   775
See how they toss their shaggy manes,
And snuff the disstant Air,
Impatient through the wave the rising Car to bear.
Now blow the Conch, loud let the joyful Sounds
Through all the rocks and hollow caverns ring,   780
And summon, from our Empire's furthest bounds,
The Race of Ocean to attend their King.
Within her Grot shall Amphitrite hear,
And in her Shell upon the wave appear:
And there around our Queen,   785
Exposing to the wanton Air
The flowing tresses of our sea-green hair,
Our numerous Bands of Nereids shall be seen.

EPODE.

GLADLY we to air ascend,
Suffering mortals to befriend :   790
And when the stormy winds are fled,
And again the Vessels spread
Their canvass wide, to catch the frolick Breeze,
That strays behind, to sport upon the seas ;
On the waters as they lie,   795
Each, beneath her crooked keel,
Our aid shall feel,
And o'er the Ocean fly,
Swift as the Sea-bird skims along the wave,
Returning to her callow brood,   800
Which, to seek her wat'ry food,
Or on the Sands she left, or in some hollow Cave.
And then the anxious Crowds,
Who on the chalky Cliffs of Albion stand,
And o'er the blue Sea throw their eager eyes,   805
Oft hailing for their ships, the fleecy clouds,
That distant in the bright Horizon rise
Shall see the white Sail glitter in the Sun,

And with loud Shouts proclaim th' approaching fleet,
Then hasten down upon the Strand,   810
Their gallant Friends to meet,
To view the Trophies they have won,
And hear the Dangers they have run.   813

BERTHIER's DREAM, AT ROME,

IN 1798.

BERTHIER's DREAM, at ROME.

ARGUMENT.

BERTHIER, after his entry into Rome, retiring to consider how he should most easily revive the memory of the heroes of the ancient republic, dreams, that he is placing a chaplet on the statue of Marcus Brutus, at a festival, held in honour of that old patriot, when a voice is heard from the image,—accounting for the assassination of Cæsar, as the plain consequence of the principles, in which the Romans were educated ; but admitting the errors of the Patriot School, its tendency to inflame ambition and pride, and the inadequacy of its influence to support man under adversity.—The voice then observes on the difference between that System and Christianity in those points, and also in respect to assassination ;— and concludes with a warning not to follow, in preference to the light of revealed religion, the examples of men, who confessedly walked in darkness.

Berthier's Dream, at Rome,

IN 1798.

Admonet in somnis et turbida terret Imago. VIRG.

THE Arts of France on Tyber's banks prevail'd,
And shouting crowds in triumph Berthier hail'd!
At length, the General from the noisy crew,
Fatigued with honours, to his couch withdrew—
There plann'd his future glories: from her tomb   5
To call the genius of Imperial Rome;
To strew the sacred Capitol with bays;
And make its walls re-echo with the praise
Of each stern patriot and enlighten'd sage,
Whose virtues grac'd a philosophic age,   10
Ere Christian Superstition had confin'd
Man's active powers and energies of mind.
Then ran his thoughts o'er many a Roman name,
Inscrib'd in blood upon the rolls of fame;

From him * who struck his brother to the ground,   15
For idly jesting on the rising mound,
To that firm band, who Cæsar's death conspir'd;
Rome's true-born sons : by whose example fir'd
French patriots gave that splendid project birth,
To drive the foes of Freedom from the earth ;   20
At once twelve hundred daggers to provide,.
And form a legion of Tyrannicide.
While thus he mus'd, before his slumbering eyes
The statue of great Brutus seem'd to rise;
It seem'd within a spacious fane to stand ;   25
About the marble image, hand in hand,
Young men and beauteous maids, a festive train,
Danc'd a light round to music's softest strain.
Himself too, in this scene, appear'd to hold.
A wreath like those in triumph worn of old ;.   30
Which on the statue's aweful brow he bound,
Then back retir'd, with reverence profound;
Anon the chaplet seem'd from off the stone
To fall—the music ceas'd,—a hollow groan
Was heard, and then these words in solemn tone: 35
(Meanwhile the temple seem'd to shake around,
And its new votary shudder'd at the sound) :

---

* Romulus.

" Cease your vain rites, nor look to ancient times
" To furnish precedent for modern crimes;
" 'Tis true, the world beheld great Cæsar bleed   40
" Beneath my arm, true, conscience own'd the deed :
" Yet think not, my example teaches you
" In regal blood the dagger to imbrue.
" Not mine the school that form'd your infant minds,
" The lights which guide them, or the law that binds.   45
" Rome from their earliest youth her children taught
" To mix her image with each rising thought,
" To worship her their idol; at her shrine
" Each softer feeling of the soul resign :
" No touch of love but towards her friend to know;   50
" Nor other hatred but against her foe :
" Her voice alone impell'd a Roman breast,
" Curs'd if she censur'd, in her praises blest ;
" Such Junius sat, and saw with stedfast eye
" The lictors hand the young offenders tie;   55
" Without a groan beheld his sons expire ;
" A genuine patriot, though a cruel sire.
" Such stern Horatius stabb'd the love-sick maid,
" Who in the public joy her grief betray'd,
" And dar'd the lustre of his triumph stain   60
" With tears of sorrow for a lover slain ;

" Such we too round the proud dictator throng'd,
" Exacting vengeance for our country wrong'd :
" Long had the blood, at sight of her foul chains,
" Boil'd with resentment in my heated veins ;   65
" Oft too some scroll, to me by name addrest,
" Rous'd every spark of manhood in my breast ;
" Doth Marcus sleep ? hath then his country's grief
" No claim from Brutus to demand relief ?
" Not so he thought, the first, thy name who bore;   70
" Wake, Brutus, and be free, or be no more.——
" What wonder then, my hand its weapon drew
" Obedient to the only law I knew ;
" That law which bade me look for good and ill,
" For vice and virtue, to my country's will;   75
" Which doom'd the man who dar'd that will enthral
" For guilt most foul of sacrilege to fall.
" Unmov'd by hate, I aim'd the deadly blow ;
" Unpitying, saw the purple current flow ;
" With awe, held up the bloody steel on high,   80
" An offering to Rome and Liberty.——
    " Such was our Roman discipline, as wise,
" Perhaps, as man in blindness could devise :
" Unknowing whither led the paths he trod,
" If child himself of chance, or work of God.   85

" But many a sage then saw, how weak a guide
" Through life's dark maze our Patriot school supplied;
" How oft from Nature drew the mind astray,
" How to ambition left and pride a prey.
" First he of men, the chief, who on the plain   90
" Could count * five thousand foes in battle slain ;
" Then slowly moving through th' admiring throng,
" The victor's car in triumph pass'd along;
" His joyful troops with praise and loud acclaim,
" Above the stars extoll'd their hero's fame ;   95
" Himself on high (his head with laurel crown'd)
" Stood up, and threw his scornful eyes around,
" As if, he look'd, some god should now descend,
" With him in arms, fit rival, to contend;
" Nor heeded he the slave, who from behind   100
" Strove back to earth to call his soaring mind ;
" Nor notic'd, as he pass'd, the clanking chain,
" And mournful wailings of the captive train,
" Lamenting loudly their unhappy fate,
" Without one hope to chear their abject state :   105

---

* Five thousand slain was the number which entitled the Roman
general to a triumph.

" Sad proof, that Fortune's anger could depress,

" As could her smile exalt to happiness.

" High swell'd our patriot souls, if glory call'd;

" Defeat subdued us, and disgrace appall'd.

" These truths I felt, when, to despair a prey,   110

" Self-wounded on the Thracian plain * I lay;

" And the last groan, that issued from my breast,

" How vain the virtue I had known, confess'd.

  " But man no more is doom'd on earth to stray,

" Involv'd in mist, and doubtful of his way :   115

" Long since the wond'ring nations saw arise

" The star of glory in the eastern skies;

" Far beam'd its rays, beyond the utmost bound

" Of Nature's reign, the gulph of death profound;

" And piercing through the clouds of thickest night   120

" To realms, till then, conceal'd from human sight,

" Disclos'd a world unknown ; where, ever blest,

" From toil and sorrow, peace and virtue rest.

" Then too was heard, his voice, whose precepts teach

" The sons of earth those bright abodes to reach;   125

" That voice which deign'd unfold Heaven's gracious plan;

" And justified the ways of God to man;

---

* Phillippi was on the Borders of Thrace.

" Bade Pride no more her meaner neighbours scorn,
" Since men in weakness, all, and sin are born;
" Bade Power be just, and Wealth in bounty flow,   130
" Or tremble at the doom of future woe;
" Bade Poverty look up, and chear'd her eyes
" With better treasures than this earth supplies;
" Bade suff'ring Virtue on her God depend
" (The world her foe, Heaven's self shall be her friend); 135
" Taught her with joy a life of toil and care,
" As the short trial of her faith, to bear;
" Nor, though the pow'rs of hell besiege her door,
" The paths of Vice for refuge to explore;
" Nor dare the cause of right by wrong defend;   140
" Nor hope, the means are hallowed by the end:
" Think'st thou, vain man! the Lord of all can need
" A murderer's sword to make a tyrant bleed?
" Could not his will annihilate his foe
" Before thy puny hand could aim the blow?   145
" Take heed, lest, while thy stubborn thoughts reject
" His grace, and treat his goodness with neglect,
" For guides preferring to his holy word,
" Poor purblind mortals, who in darkness err'd,

" (Of whom the wisest * and the best, alone   150

" This knowledge gain'd, that nothing he had known)

" The God, whose milder voice thou would'st not hear,

" May speak in sounds of thunder to thine ear;

" And in thy punishment to sin declare,

" His arm can reach, though long his mercies spare.   155

---

* Socrates.

T. Burton, Printer,
Little Queen-street.

www.ingramcontent.com/pod-product-compliance
Lightning Source LLC
Chambersburg PA
CBHW022024080426
42733CB00007B/720